Under the Sea
Squids

by Jody Sullivan Rake

Consulting Editor: Gail Saunders-Smith, PhD

Consultant: Debbie Nuzzolo
Education Manager
SeaWorld, San Diego, California

Capstone
press®

Mankato, Minnesota

Pebble Plus is published by Capstone Press,
151 Good Counsel Drive, P.O. Box 669, Mankato, Minnesota 56002.
www.capstonepress.com

1 2 3 4 5 6 11 10 09 08 07 06

Library of Congress Cataloging-in-Publication Data
Rake, Jody Sullivan.
    Squids / by Jody Sullivan Rake.
    p. cm.—(Pebble Plus. Under the sea)
    Summary: "Simple text and photographs present the lives of squids"—Provided by publisher.
    Includes bibliographical references and index.
    ISBN-13: 978-0-7368-6367-4 (hardcover)
    ISBN-10: 0-7368-6367-2 (hardcover)
1. Squids—Juvenile literature. I. Title. II. Series: Under the sea (Mankato, Minn.)
QL430.2.R35 2007
594'.58—dc22   2005035970

Editorial Credits
Mari Schuh, editor; Juliette Peters, set designer; Patrick D. Dentinger, book designer; Kelly Garvin,
    photo researcher/photo editor

Photo Credits
Bruce Coleman Inc./Jeff Foott, 20–21
Nature Picture Library/David Shale, 12–13
PhotoDisc Inc., back cover
Seapics/Bob Cranston, 14–15; David B. Fleetham, 9; Doc White, 10–11; Doug Perrine, 17; James D. Watt, 4–5;
    Jeff Jaskolski, cover; Masa Ushioda, 1; Richard Herrmann, 7, 18–19

Note to Parents and Teachers

The Under the Sea set supports national science standards related to the diversity and
unity of life. This book describes and illustrates squids. The images support early readers
in understanding the text. The repetition of words and phrases helps early readers learn
new words. This book also introduces early readers to subject-specific vocabulary words,
which are defined in the Glossary section. Early readers may need assistance to read
some words and to use the Table of Contents, Glossary, Read More, Internet Sites, and
Index sections of the book.

Table of Contents

What Are Squids?

Squids are ocean animals.
Their soft bodies
have no bones.

Most squids are

as long as a watermelon.

Some squids are

much longer than a bus.

Body Parts

Squids have two big eyes.

Squids can see very well

in the ocean.

A tube called a siphon

sticks out near a squid's head.

Squids squirt water

through siphons

to zoom through the ocean.

siphon

Ten tentacles are around
a squid's mouth.
Suckers on the tentacles
help squids grab prey.

What Squids Do

Squids catch and eat
fish and shrimp
with their long tentacles.

Squids change color to hide.

Squids also change color

to talk to each other.

Squids squirt clouds of ink.

The ink makes it hard

for predators to see.

Then the squids

can get away.

Under the Sea

Squids swim together
in large groups
under the sea.

Glossary

ink—a colored liquid that makes a cloud in the water

predator—an animal that hunts other animals for food

prey—an animal that is eaten by another animal; fish and shrimp are prey of squids.

siphon—a tube on a squid's body that moves liquids; siphons help squids swim quickly through the water.

squirt—to send out a stream of liquid from a small opening

sucker—a body part on squids that sticks to surfaces and to other animals

tentacle—a squid's long flexible arm; squids use their tentacles to move, feel, and grab.

Read More

Hirschmann, Kris. *Squid.* Creatures of the Sea. San Diego: Kidhaven Press, 2004.

Knox, Barbara. *ABC Under the Sea: An Ocean life Alphabet Book.* Alphabet Books. Mankato, Minn.: A+ Books, 2003.

Redmond, Shirley-Raye. *Tentacles!: Tales of the Giant Squid.* Step into Reading. New York: Random House, 2003.

Internet Sites

FactHound offers a safe, fun way to find Internet sites related to this book. All of the sites on FactHound have been researched by our staff.

Here's how:

1. Visit *www.facthound.com*

2. Choose your grade level.

3. Type in this book ID **0736863672** for age-appropriate sites. You may also browse subjects by clicking on letters, or by clicking on pictures and words.

4. Click on the **Fetch It** button.

FactHound will fetch the best sites for you!

Index

Word Count: 129
Grade: 1
Early-Intervention Level: 14